DARE TO BE FREE!

How many people do you know who are free?

Truly free. Not just free from external restraints—from prison bars or oppressive governments. But free from the inside out. Free from sickness and disease, free from depression and fear, free from poverty and lack, free from the pain and unforgiveness of the past.

How many people do you know who have that kind of joyous liberty?

Odds are, you don't know more than one or two…if that many. The reason is simple. Despite all the talk about freedom these days, most people are more bound and trapped than ever before.

You may even be feeling that way yourself right now. Maybe you're a Christian—you've asked Jesus to come into your heart and be Lord of your life—and you know you should be enjoying the freedom the Bible teaches. But for some reason, you're stuck, unable to shake loose from the devilish circumstances, habits or afflictions that keep you chained.

If so, I want you to know—I understand. I've been there. I know what it's like to be born again and baptized in the Holy Spirit, yet living in the blackest darkness imaginable. I know what it is to be so tormented that death seemed the only escape.

I also know what it is like to take the weapon God has given each one of us and fight my way through to freedom.

And I know if I can do it...you can do it too.

MORE THAN A SUNDAY MORNING DOSE

What is this weapon I'm talking about? Jesus reveals it to us in John 8:31-32. There He says:

...If you abide in My word [hold fast to My teachings and live in accordance with them], you are truly My disciples. And you

LYNNE HAMMOND

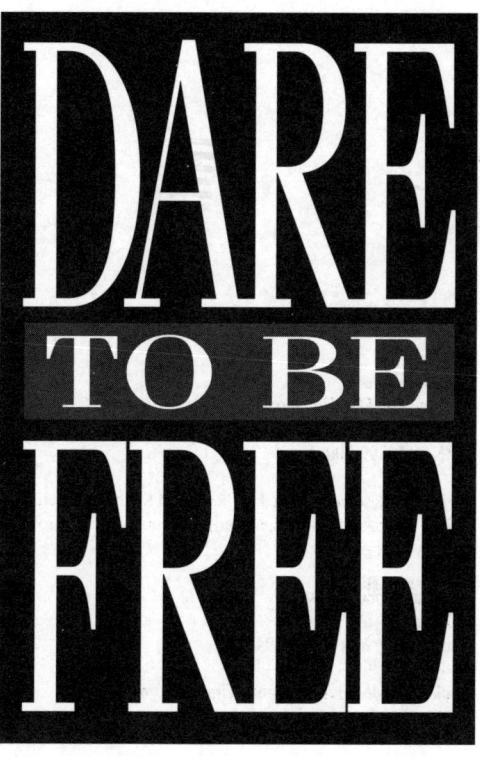

DARE TO BE FREE

Dare to Be Free!
Published by Mac Hammond Ministries
© 1994 Mac Hammond Ministries
ISBN: 1-57399-000-0

All Rights Reserved. Printed in the United States of America.
Unless otherwise indicated, all scripture quotations are from
the ©Amplified Bible.

Mac Hammond Ministries
P.O. Box 29469
Minneapolis, MN 55429-2946

Book cover design/production: Virgil B. Lynn
Be-Graphic, Inc., Oklahoma City, Oklahoma

will know the Truth, and the Truth will set you free.

The truth of God, which is His Word, is the only weapon powerful enough to blast through any wall of bondage. It is the only thing that will set you free and keep you free.

Read the last phrase of that verse again. *The truth will set you free.* Notice it doesn't say your pastor will set you free. It doesn't say your psychologist will set you free. It doesn't say your doctor will set you free. It doesn't say singing and dancing is going to set you free. It doesn't even say prayer is going to set you free.

It says the only thing that will ever set you totally free is the Word of the living God.

You may be thinking, "Well, I go to church on Sunday and hear the Word. I read my Bible. But I'm not free."

That's not surprising. I have found that a Sunday morning dose of the Word isn't enough. An occasional Bible reading isn't enough. If I want to be truly free, I have to apply the Word of God to my life every day. I have to do what God instructed Joshua to do when He said:

This Book of the Law shall not depart out of your mouth, but you shall meditate on it day and night, that you may observe and do according to all that is written in it. For then you shall make your way prosperous, and then you shall deal wisely and have good success. (Joshua 1:8)

Some people say it's impossible to stay in the Word day and night. But I can tell you it's not, because that's what I did for nine long months. In fact, there was a period in my life when I often spent 16 to 18 hours a day reading and meditating on the Word of God.

Why did I spend that much time? Because I was that desperate.

Don't panic. Unless you're in the kind of life-and-death situation I was facing, you won't have to spend that many hours to find your freedom. In fact, the Word of God is so powerful that if you were simply to commit to it the amount of time you probably waste on useless amusements each day, you'd step into the most wonderful life of liberty you've ever known.

SUPERNATURAL MEDICINE

How can I be so sure that's true?

There are two reasons. The first is because the Bible says so. It tells us:

> ...*The Word that God speaks is alive and full of power [making it active, operative, energizing, and effective]; it is sharper than any two-edged sword, penetrating to the dividing line of the breath of life (soul) and [the immortal] spirit, and of joints and marrow [of the deepest parts of our nature], exposing and sifting and analyzing and judging the very thoughts and purposes of the heart. (Hebrews 4:12)*

The Word of God isn't just a bunch of ideas in a leather-bound book. The Word of God is alive. It has life in it!

People everywhere are looking for life. But most of them are looking in the wrong places. Some folks think exercise will give them life, so they spend all their time at the health club. Others seem to think food is going to give them life, so they center their lives around eating. Still others have the idea that relaxing will give them life. So they spend every possible moment on vacation.

But the reality is, even though each of those things has its place, none of them can give you life. There's only one place you can go to get life and that is the Word of God!

You see, the Word of God contains the very substance of God Himself. It's not just nice-sounding phrases. It is actual spiritual substance.

When you get your Bible out and begin to read and meditate the Word, the Holy Spirit imparts that substance to you. You partake of the very life and nature of God Himself. (See 2 Peter 1:4).

I'm not talking about just a mental effect or a little spiritual influence. I'm saying that as you receive God's Word, His power is transmitted to you. And that power will change anything that needs changing in your life.

You may think, "Well, I just can't understand how that can be. I can't see how God's Word can affect me in a real, physical way."

Sure you can! Think about the last time you went to the doctor and got a prescription for an illness. You may have felt terribly sick. You may not have had the slightest idea how that medication was supposed to work. Yet you had no doubt that by swallowing those little round pills, your body would be changed. You fully believed they had a substance within them that would make you well.

The Words of God work much the same way. They are God's medicine. Proverbs says "they are life to those who find them, and health (or medicine) to all their flesh."

And the great thing about God's medicine is it never, ever fails.

"JESUS IS YOUR ONLY ANSWER."

As I said before, there are two reasons I can be sure of that. One, because the Word says so. And, two, because at a time when doctors, psychiatrists, and medicines could not help me—the Word of God saved my life.

I was a new Christian when it happened. I'd only been born again and baptized in the Holy

Spirit a few months. I had so little knowledge of the Bible that I asked Jesus to come into my heart every day for the first three months I was saved. I just didn't know any better!

All my life I'd been a happy, outgoing person. Add to that the delight of discovering Jesus and you can imagine how full of joy I was.

Then, suddenly, all that changed.

Overnight the Devil came into my life like a flood. Darkness closed in around my mind. Depression set in that was so deep and terrifying, it often left me in a trance. Bleeding ulcers racked my body and reduced me to little more than skin and bones.

Physically, I was so weak that I couldn't be left alone. I remember once when simply walking down the hall to my baby daughter's bedroom in answer to her cry so drained me of strength that I fell repeatedly. Once I reached her bed, I collapsed upon it unable to move without help.

Like cancer of the mind, mental illness began to eat away at my sanity. Thoughts of suicide and screaming demonic voices hounded me day and night. At times, my central nervous system broke down under the pressure of it. When that happened, it was as if all of my inward parts were shattering and all I wanted to do was die.

The doctors diagnosed me as "manic depressive," moving over into schizophrenia and hallucinations at times. My once boisterous, outgoing personality had vanished, leaving me timid and shy. Confusion so clouded my mind that, at times, I would answer the phone, then forget I was having a conversation and simply lay the receiver down and walk away.

There were no pills that would help. Nothing anyone could do.

Thank God, my clinical psychologist was a Spirit-filled Christian. And he told me the truth. "Jesus is your only answer."

SUPERNATURAL SHOCK TREATMENT

Although I didn't know much about spiritual things back then, I did know one thing. The way to get to Jesus was through the Word of God.

So I started reading the Word. I followed the

instructions in James 1:21 which says, "Get rid of all uncleanness and the rampant outgrowth of wickedness, and in a humble (gentle, modest) spirit receive and welcome the Word which implanted and rooted [in your hearts] contains the power to save your souls."

That's what I needed—power to save my soul. Because I was born again, my spirit was already saved. But my soul (my mind, will and emotions) was desperately ill and I needed to be delivered.

One thing you need to understand is this. When I say I started reading the Word, I don't mean I had a 15-minute daily devotional time. I spent every possible moment reading and quoting the Word. Sometimes I would read it all night because I couldn't sleep.

Other times, when the ulcers in my stomach would cause me to vomit repeatedly, I would take my Bible with me into the bathroom. Then, in between bouts of sickness I would speak the Word saying, "Man shall not live by bread alone, but by every word that proceeds out of the mouth of God" (Matthew 4:4).

Even that, however, was not enough.

You see, every thought I had all day long was evil. The Bible says, "...whatsoever things are true, whatsoever things are honest, whatsoever things are just, whatsoever things are pure, whatsoever things are lovely, whatsoever things are of good report; if there be any virtue, and if there be any praise, think on these things" (Philippians 4:8). Yet none of my thoughts fell into any of those categories!

I knew somehow I had to change that. I knew I had to do something dramatic enough to jolt my mind out of those demonic thought patterns. So here's what I did. I put a rubber band around my wrist. (That's right, a rubber band! Not the big kind, either, but the thin kind that stings when it snaps against your skin.) Then, every time a thought came to me that was not the Word of God, I'd pull that rubber band back and snap myself on the wrist.

When the Devil would come to me and say, "You're going to commit suicide today"—which he did hundreds of times a day—I'd pop my wrist with that rubber band as hard as I could.

Then I'd say, "No, in the name of Jesus Christ, I tread upon scorpions and serpents and I have power over all the enemy" (Luke 10:19).

After the first four or five hours of the day, my wrists would be raw and bleeding. But eventually, my mind would start turning away from those evil thoughts instead of entertaining them. I'd refuse to have them because I remembered how bad that popping hurt and I didn't want to experience it again.

I realize that may sound extreme to you. It *was* extreme. But I was facing an extremely critical situation.

Later, when I told my psychologist what I had done, he said, "You know what you were doing don't you? You were giving yourself shock treatment."

I had no idea at the time that's what I was doing. I only knew that it worked because after only one month of it, I began to have days when the darkness would clear away, days when all that depression, all those mountains of frustration, all the suicidal pressure would lift and I would be free.

MEDITATION X 3 = VICTORY!

But I want you to know, on those wonderful days, I didn't celebrate by going shopping or going to the movies. No, I'd spend those good days meditating the Word of God. I would arm myself with it so I'd be prepared for the next attack.

Since that time, I've discovered that although the Bible says a great deal about meditating on the Word, very few Christians actually know how to do that. So let me share with you the three ways that worked for me.

First, when I would get up in the morning, I would read the Word—not large portions of it but just short sections. I would pick out one particular word in that passage of scripture that seemed to speak especially to my heart. For example, I might read Psalm 91:2, "I will say of the Lord, He is my refuge and my fortress: my God; in him will I trust." Then I would take the word *refuge*, get out my concordance and cross reference it, reading every scriptural reference to *refuge* throughout the Bible.

Then I would think all day (and many times

all night) about the fact that God is my refuge.

I'd also meditate the Word by vividly imagining, and even acting out, individual Bible stories. One of my favorites was the story in Mark 10 about the blind beggar, Bartimaeus. There, beginning in verse 46, the Bible says:

> *As (Jesus) was leaving Jericho with His disciples and a great crowd, Bartimaeus, a blind beggar, a son of Timaeus, was sitting by the roadside. And when he heard that is was Jesus of Nazareth, he began to shout, saying, Jesus, Son of David, have pity and mercy on me [now]! And many severely censured and reproved him, telling him to keep still, but he kept on shouting out all the more, You Son of David, have pity and mercy on me [now]! And Jesus stopped and said, Call him. And they called the blind man, telling him, Take courage! Get up! He is calling you. And throwing off his outer garment, he leaped up and came to Jesus. And Jesus said to him, What do you want Me to do for you? And the blind man said to Him, Master,*

let me receive my sight. And Jesus said to him, go your way; your faith has healed you. And at once he received his sight and accompanied Jesus on the road.

I didn't just read that story, I lived it. I would picture Jericho in my mind. I'd see Jesus walking with His disciples and the crowds gathered all around. I'd imagine how Bartimaeus felt as he frantically cried out to get Jesus' attention, and I'd hear the voices of the people around him as they scolded him saying, "Be quiet, Bartimaeus! Who do you think you are? Keep your mouth shut!"

I studied and found out that in those days people who were blind had to wear an outer garment around them, a yellow cloak that labeled them *"blind."* In that way, I identified with Bartimaeus. The doctors had labeled me "manic depressive." In essence, I too was wearing a cloak.

So, taking the part of Bartimaeus, I would act out that story. I would sit down on the floor and envision myself sitting by the roadside in Jericho. Then I would say, "Son of David, have mercy on me! Son of David, have mercy on me!"

In my mind's eye, I would see Jesus calling me to Him. And do you know what I would do next?

I would jump up and throw off that label of "manic depressive" just like Bartimaeus stood up and threw off that yellow cloak of blindness—and I would see myself free!

The third way I would meditate the Word was by taking a whole verse of scripture and carry it with me all day long. I don't mean I'd put a Bible in my purse and carry it with me. I mean, I'd put that scripture in my mind and heart and just think about it night and day, turning it over and over in my mind.

You didn't know meditating the Word was so much work, did you? Sure, it takes effort but it's the most richly rewarding effort you'll ever put forth. For me, it was worth every moment because after less than nine months of that kind of meditation I was totally free.

Just think, if I could be delivered from that kind of hopeless situation in just nine months, how long would it take you to get a breakthrough in your life? A few weeks? A day or two?

Would it be worth the effort? Yes, yes, yes!

"YE ARE MIGHTY!"

There is one important thing about applying the Word, however, that you must understand. For its power to be fully activated in your life, you must use it like a mirror. You must look into it, see who it says you are and—despite all natural appearances to the contrary—you must believe it! And once you believe it, you must act on it!

That is vital to your breakthrough. James 1:22-25 puts it this way:

But be doers of the Word [obey the message], and not merely listeners to it, betraying yourselves [into deception...]. For if anyone only listens to the Word without obeying it and being a doer of it, he is like a man who looks carefully at his [own] natural face in a mirror; For he thoughtfully observes himself, and then goes off and promptly forgets what he was like. But he who looks carefully into the faultless law of liberty, and is faithful to it and perseveres in looking into it, being not a heedless listener who forgets but an active doer [who obeys], he shall be blessed in his doing...

I'll never forget when I first learned the truth of that scripture. I had been battling that mental illness for many months. It was the end of February and I almost had the victory.

Throughout that illness, there had been times when darkness would come over me in an overwhelming way. At those times, I could hear a host of demons coming toward me and I knew when they reached me the torment was going to be so great I could hardly bear it.

I wasn't demon possessed, but I was demon obsessed and oppressed. When they attacked me in that way it felt as though they were pecking my brains out. They would scream inside my head with the loudest screams you ever heard. Immediately I would go into a trance and lay stiff as a board in my bed, unable to move.

In the early days of my fight of faith, I would hear the voice of God at those times. He would say, "Praise Me."

I felt so unable to do that, sometimes I would just put the pillow over my head. But then God would speak to me again. "Lift your hands and praise Me!"

Do you know why He told me to do that? Because of what it says in Psalm 8:2. "Out of the mouths of babes and unweaned infants You have established strength [or praise, as Jesus put it in Matthew 21:15] because of Your foes, that You might silence the enemy and the avenger."

Praise stills the enemy!

So I would try it. I was so weak it would take every ounce of my strength pushing as hard as I could to lift my arms and say, "Praise You, Lord." But I did it and I found that by the time I said "Praise You" 25 times, the Devil always left!

For seven months, that's all I knew to get me through those horrible attacks. Then one day, the Lord began saying something new to me. It seemed to me a very strange thing to say at the time. When those demon powers would try to come rushing in on me, He would tell me, *"Ye are mighty. Isn't that true?"*

I can tell you, I didn't feel mighty. There I was, a little, puny woman, lying in the bed wanting to pull the covers over my head. I seemed the very picture of weakness. Yet over and over, the Lord would speak to my heart and say, *"Ye are mighty. Isn't that true?"*

He wanted me to agree with Him but I just couldn't. As I was meditating that scripture passage in James one day, however, suddenly I realized what I was doing wrong. I realized that I had been looking in the Bible, reading that I was mighty in the Lord, reading that I was an overcomer and more than a conqueror. But when I shut the book and walked away from that mirror of the Word, I would forget what kind of person I was in Jesus.

I would forget that I was mighty!

Once I understood that, I saw what the Lord was trying to get me to do. He was wanting me to believe and act like I was mighty—regardless of my feelings.

When I got that revelation, it was all over for the Devil. I determined that every time he sent that demon hoard my way, I was going to leap to my feet, grab my Bible and act like the "Mighty Man" I was. I determined I was going to quote the Word and put that Devil under my feet. I was going to make him pay for every moment he spent in my presence.

I did it too. And do you know what? It wasn't long before he quit coming. It wasn't long before he fled in total defeat!

CUT THE DEVIL TO SHREDS

Maybe you aren't facing exactly the situation I was facing. Maybe today, you're fighting the battle of faith on a different front. Maybe the Devil is trying to steal your finances or your marriage, your physical health or your children.

I know one thing for sure, he is trying to steal *something* from you because he is a thief by nature; and the Bible tells us the thief comes to kill, steal and destroy (John 10:10).

He'll do it too, if you're not mighty. He'll

take everything you'll let him have. He'll put you in bondage then he'll keep you there, if you don't resist him.

So start resisting him today!

Get the Word of God and begin to meditate on it. Speak it. Pray it. Think on it. Act it out if necessary. Do whatever you need to do to get that Word rooted solidly in your heart.

Then rise up, take that Sword of the Spirit and cut the Devil to threads with it. You may *feel* like running for cover. You may *feel* like hiding under the bed. But don't do that.

Instead, remember, *Ye are mighty!*

Believe it. Act on it. For it is the truth and the truth will make you free!

PRAYER FOR SALVATION AND BAPTISM IN THE HOLY SPIRIT

God in Heaven, I come to You in the name of Your Son, Jesus. I confess that I haven't lived my life for You, but I am glad to know that I can change that. Your Word says "whosoever shall call on the name of the Lord shall be saved" (Acts 2:21). I am calling on You. I believe that Jesus is the Son of God. I believe that He died on the cross and rose again from the dead so I might have a better life now and eternal life in heaven. Jesus, come into my heart and be my Lord and Savior. In Jesus' name I pray. Amen.

I am now reborn! I am a Christian—a child of God. I am saved! You also said in Your Word, "If ye then, being evil, know how to give good gifts unto your children: HOW MUCH MORE shall your heavenly father give the Holy Spirit to them that ask Him?" (Luke 11:13) I'm also asking you to baptize me with the Holy Spirit. Holy Spirit, rise up within me as I praise God. I fully expect to speak with other tongues as You give me the utterance (Acts 2:4).

(Begin to praise God for filling you with the Holy Spirit. Speak those words and syllables you receive— not in English. You have to use your own voice. God will not force you to speak.)

Now you are a Spirit-filled believer. Continue with the blessing God has given you and pray in tongues each day. From this day forward, to the best of your ability and by the power of the Holy Spirit, live your life for God.

OTHER BOOKS AVAILABLE FROM MAC HAMMOND MINISTRIES

BOOKS BY MAC HAMMOND

Living Safely—Keys to Abiding in the Secret Place

Heirs Together—Solving the Mystery of a Satisfying Marriage

Real Faith Never Fails—Detecting (and Correcting) Four Common Faith Mistakes

The Way of the Winner—Running the Race to Victory

Water, Wind & Fire—Understanding the New Birth and the Baptism of the Holy Spirit

Winning the World—Becoming the Bold Soul Winner God Created You to Be

For more information about this ministry or a complete catalog of teaching tapes and other materials available, please write:

Mac Hammond Ministries
P.O. Box 29469
Minneapolis, MN 55429-2946